W9-BHZ-863

DISCARDED BY THE
URBANA FREE LIBRARY

DATE DUE

DEC 0 6 2009
DEC 17 2002   JAN 28 2008
FEB 14 2004   JUL 16 2013
          FEB 16 2003
                    DEC 04 2012
    JUL 30 2005
M MAR 19 2006
    MAY 22 2007
DEC 17 2007

URBANA FREE LIBRARY
CHILDREN'S DEPARTMENT
(217) 367-4069

• • THE LIBRARY OF FAMOUS WOMEN • •

JANE GOODALL

Naturalist

by
J. A. Senn

A BLACKBIRCH PRESS BOOK

WOODBRIDGE, CONNECTICUT

j 591
BIO
Goodall
Cop. 1
11-93-BT-15.00

Published by Blackbirch Press, Inc.
One Bradley Road, Suite 205
Woodbridge, CT 06525

©1993 Blackbirch Press, Inc.
First Edition

All rights reserved. No part of this book may be reproduced in any form without permission in writing from Blackbirch Press, Inc., except by a reviewer.

Manufactured in the United States

10 9 8 7 6 5 4 3 2 1

Library of Congress Cataloging-in-Publication Data

Senn, J. A.
    Jane Goodall, friend of the chimpanzee/by J.A. Senn—1st ed.
      p.   cm. — (The Library of famous women)
    Includes bibliographical references and index.
    Summary: Examines the personal and professional life of the noted zoologist and describes her work with the chimpanzees of Tanzania.
    ISBN 0-56711-010-X
    1. Goodall, Jane, 1934-   —Juvenile literature. 2. Chimpanzees—Tanzania—Gombe Stream National Park—Juvenile literature. 3. Primatologists—England—Biography—Juvenile literature. [1. Goodall, Jane, 1934– 2. Zoologists. 3. Chimpanzees.] I. Title. II. Series.
QL31.G58S46 1993
599.8'092—dc20
[B]   93-1223
                                                  CIP
                                                      AC

Contents

Introduction

Jane Goodall has spent more than 30 years in Africa, where she has devoted all her time to studying chimpanzees. Before she began her life's work, no one knew much about these animals. But Jane's hard work has led to important discoveries.

Many people believe that she has saved the African chimpanzees from dying out. Because of her books and reports, African officials have set aside land for the chimps. This book is about Jane Goodall's extraordinary life and her great love for these amazing creatures.

(Opposite page) **Jane Goodall has spent more than 30 years working with chimpanzees at the Gombe Stream Game Reserve in Africa. Many believe her hard work has helped to save African chimpanzees from extinction.**

5

(Opposite page)
The chimps at Gombe have become so used to Jane that they no longer feel threatened by her. Many, in fact, see her as one of their own.

One of these creatures, in particular, was probably responsible for inspiring Jane to stay in Africa for as long as she did. The story begins on a Christmas day—Jane's very first Christmas at the Gombe Stream Game Reserve in Africa.

As was often the case, Jane walked deep into the forest that morning. She followed a path commonly traveled by groups of chimpanzees. Unlike other mornings, however, this time Jane stopped to decorate a small tree along her way. Reaching deep into the pockets of her tan shorts, she pulled out little bits of silver paper and round fluffy balls of cotton. After she had put them all over the tree, she laid an extra-large supply of bananas underneath it. The bananas were her Christmas present to the chimpanzees. She sat down near the tree and began to wait.

A little while later, Goliath and William, two large chimpanzees, arrived. When they saw the bananas, they shouted loudly with surprise. They threw their arms around each other and danced excitedly. Finally, they sat down to eat their Christmas feast. As they ate, they made little happy grunts and squeaks.

Then, David Graybeard, another large male chimpanzee, arrived. When he saw

the bananas, he also sat down and began to eat eagerly. Knowing that David was a particularly calm and gentle animal, Jane quietly moved over beside him. She sat very still for a long time. Then, slowly, she moved her hand toward David's shoulder, and she made a grooming movement.

Grooming is an important activity among chimpanzees. During grooming, chimps carefully part the hairs of other chimps and pick off little flakes of dried skin, grass seed, or small bugs.

When Jane first touched David, he gently pushed her hand away. After waiting a little while, she tried again. This time he let her groom him for about a minute. Jane was thrilled. A wild chimpanzee let her—a human being—*touch* him! She had never had such a wonderful Christmas present.

Years later, she told her husband about her first Christmas at the chimpanzee reserve. "You know," she said, "chimps have so many emotions just like us. And yet we are so much smarter than they are."

"Yes," her husband replied, "chimps really aren't animals. Of course, they really aren't people either. They are just some strange and very wonderful in-between creatures."

❖

A wild chimpanzee had let her—a human being— touch him! She had never had such a wonderful Christmas present.

Chapter 1

An Invitation to Africa

Jane Goodall was born in London, England, on April 3, 1934. One of her earliest memories is very sad and made a lasting impression on her. She once saw a man kill a dragonfly. She remembers crying for a long time after it happened. Later she said, "I felt bad that such a pretty thing was destroyed."

A Love of Animals

Jane's mother quickly recognized her daughter's love of all creatures—a love that would continue throughout Jane's life. When Jane was very young, Mrs. Goodall presented her daughter with Jubilee, a stuffed chimpanzee toy. It soon became Jane's favorite traveling companion—she took it everywhere she went. Even today, many years later, Jubilee is still one of Jane's most cherished possessions.

When Jane was five, she and her family moved to a city near the English Channel. She loved her new home. She could ride horses and spend hours watching insects and animals. Later she recalled, "I did well in school, but I always wanted to be outside watching and learning."

Once Jane hid in a small, stuffy henhouse for five hours. She wanted to see how chickens laid eggs. When she finally got home, she learned that everyone had been worried about her. Her mother, however, was not angry. She was happy that Jane had such a strong interest in animals.

When Jane was seven years old, she read *The Story of Dr. Dolittle*, a book about an Englishman who lived in Africa. But this man had a very unusual ability. He could talk to all the animals. "I think that's when I first decided that someday I had to go to Africa," Jane later recalled.

On to Kenya

After she graduated from high school, Jane went back to London. There she studied to be a secretary. She had decided to become a secretary for one reason. Her mother had told her that a secretary could get a job anywhere in the world, and she was still determined to go to Africa.

Jane Goodall's World

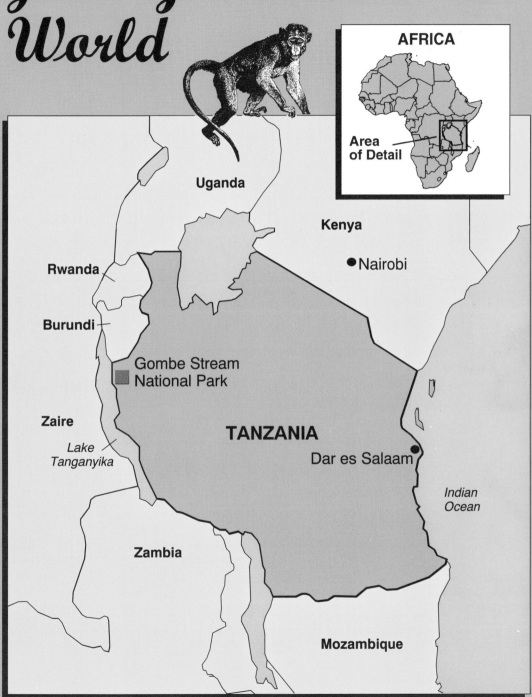

AFRICA

Area of Detail

Uganda

Kenya

●Nairobi

Rwanda

Burundi

Gombe Stream
National Park

Zaire

TANZANIA

Lake
Tanganyika

Dar es Salaam●

Indian
Ocean

Zambia

Mozambique

Jane did become a secretary, and she worked in London for several years. One day when she returned to her apartment, she found a letter with a postmark from Africa. It was from a school friend of hers. Her friend explained that she was now living in Kenya with her parents. The best part of the letter, however, came at the end. It was an invitation for Jane to go visit them in Africa.

Jane was so excited that the next day she quit her job and moved back with her parents. She knew she would not be able to save money fast enough in London. Everything there cost too much. At home, she got a job as a waitress and saved every cent she could. Soon she had enough money to buy a ticket on a passenger line heading for Africa. At age 23, Jane was finally on her way to fulfilling her dream.

"If you like animals so much," her friend said, "then you should meet Dr. Leakey."

Meeting Dr. Leakey

After staying with her friend in Kenya for a couple of weeks, Jane accepted a job as a secretary in Nairobi, the capital of Kenya. One day she told a friend how much she liked animals. "If you like animals so much," her friend said, "then you should meet Dr. Leakey. He studies the bones of dead animals."

On her next day off, Jane went to the National Museum of Natural History to meet Dr. Louis Leakey. After talking to her for just a short while, Dr. Leakey could sense Jane's great love for animals. He was so impressed that he immediately asked her to work for him. Jane happily accepted.

For the next several months, Jane worked with Dr. Leakey and his wife. Each day they would dig for the bones of animals that had lived millions of years ago. "It was interesting work," Jane recalls. "But I still wanted to study living animals. I wanted to come as close to talking to animals as I could. I still wanted to be like Dr. Dolittle."

Jane's most important teacher was Dr. Louis Leakey, a world-famous researcher in Africa. It was Dr. Leakey who first suggested that Jane study chimpanzees in Tanzania.

The best part of each day for Jane was when everyone walked back to camp. Jane was always last because she would stop and watch the animals. She loved to watch as the small antelopes rushed by. Sometimes she could even catch a glimpse of a herd of giraffes off in the distance.

Jane's interest in animals became more and more obvious to Dr. Leakey as time went on. Knowing that Jane's interest should not go to waste, he began to speak with her about a particular group of chimpanzees that had never before had any contact with human beings. He thought someone should study them. He told Jane, "It may soon be too late to study these chimps. People are getting closer and closer to where they live. Soon they will kill the chimps and take over the land."

A New Job

Dr. Leakey stressed how important the study of the chimps would be. "I think the chimpanzees can tell us a lot about the habits of prehistoric people," he told her. He paused for a minute. Then he asked her if she wanted a job studying the chimps. Jane could hardly believe what she was hearing. This was exactly the kind of job she had always dreamed about!

Jane returned to England to get ready for her new job. Shortly thereafter, she received word that the African government had given her permission to go to the Gombe Stream Game Reserve to study the chimpanzees. She was, however, not allowed to go alone. Her first volunteer was her mother, Vanne Goodall.

In 1960, Jane, her mother, their cook and his wife, and a government official headed up Lake Tanganyika to the chimpanzee reserve in Tanzania, a country just below Kenya. As the boat slowly chugged along, Jane watched the shore. She saw steep

Jane first ventured down Africa's Lake Tanganyika (*below*) in 1960. Her destination was the Gombe Stream Game Reserve in Tanzania, where she studied chimps for the next 30 years.

mountains that rose up almost out of the water. In between the slopes there were dense tropical forests that ran into narrow valleys. To observe the chimps, she would have to find her way through these thick, overgrown rain forests.

After a two-hour ride, the group finally arrived. David Anstey, the government official, introduced some of the natives and tried to help the team get its bearings. The heat was so brutal that Jane thought she might pass out.

As soon as everything was set up, Jane slipped away. She wanted to explore the area around the camp. Even though it was four o'clock, the sun was still hot. As a result, Jane was covered with sweat by the time she had climbed a high ridge. At the top, however, she was able to see the lake and the surrounding mountains. As she sat there, a troop of about 60 baboons hurried by. When they noticed her, some gave her a loud alarm bark, but most of the others did not seem bothered by her presence.

That night Jane pulled her cot out of the tent so she could sleep under the stars. "I remember that night very clearly," she later wrote. "I didn't feel like an intruder anymore. I felt like I belonged."

Chapter 2

The Beginning

The next day two local guides led Jane through the forest to a huge tree. Hanging from the tree's branches were hundreds of orange and red fruits. Underneath it, Jane saw many broken branches and pieces of chewed-fruit remains. "Chimpanzees were here yesterday eating the fruit. They will come back again today," one of the guides explained.

Learning Her Way Around

Jane was eager to learn whatever she could about the chimpanzees, but she also needed to learn patience. Choosing a spot across from the tree that the guides had taken her to, she sat and waited. Soon she heard the hooting sounds that chimpanzees make. Then she caught a glimpse of 16 chimpanzees as they climbed into the tree. To her great delight, one of them was a mother chimp with a tiny baby holding onto her stomach.

The chimps stayed in the tree for about two hours. Jane's excitement soon turned to disappointment, however. She was able to see only a hand or a little piece of an arm among the thick leaves of the tree. That was all that was visible.

Then, just as quickly as they had come, the chimpanzees left. And they left in complete silence! "That's what amazed me the most," Jane remarked. "There were sixteen chimpanzees in one tree. And yet the only sounds I heard had been the calls announcing their arrival."

Over the next 10 days, different groups of chimpanzees visited the same tree. Twice Jane tried to move closer to the tree so that she could see more. But each time she did, the chimps ran away. Then one day the fruit was gone, and the chimps stopped going to the tree altogether.

For the next two months, Jane rarely saw a chimp. She and her guides searched for another fruit tree but never found one. When they did come across some chimps by accident, the chimps ran away. Jane became discouraged—she worried that she would never get close enough to the chimps to learn anything.

Later, however, Jane realized that those early weeks were not a total loss. She had begun to learn her way around the area. Her skin had become hardened against the rough grasses, and tsetse-fly bites no longer made her sick. She also had learned the different animal tracks. Most of all, she had grown so accustomed to the forest that she was at ease, and she could walk quickly.

When she first arrived in Africa, Jane faced many hardships and obstacles. After only a short while, however, she settled in and made a permanent home among the chimpanzees of the Gombe Reserve.

A Setback

Three months after Jane and her mother arrived, they became very ill with malaria. Government officials had told Jane not to worry about malaria, because it comes from the bite of certain mosquitoes only. They had also assured her that none of those mosquitoes were in her area.

As the malaria got worse, Jane and her mother ran fevers of up to 105 degrees F.! They became very hot and sweaty. Then they got terrible chills. Hot and cold, hot and cold—for five days. They could not eat; they could do nothing but lie on their cots in the tent.

One night when Jane's mother was very sick, she wandered out of the tent alone. It was as if she were in a dream—falling in and out of consciousness. Luckily, Dominic, the cook, found her before she hurt herself and helped her back into her tent. After 10 days, both women were finally feeling better. But many people later told them how lucky they had been to pull through at all.

Although there was no medicine for malaria, Jane's mother had brought other medicines with her. She had wanted to open a clinic for the local people. Soon she did exactly that.

Jane figured that most people who came to the clinic when it first opened were not sick at all, but just curious to see the two Englishwomen who had come to study the chimpanzees. Over time, however, Vanne's clinic did help many people. In fact, some walked over the mountains to come to her. Jane later wrote, "The Africans continued to think we were both slightly crazy. But they were friendly when they realized we were sincere."

Jane loved having her mother with her. Years later, in *In the Shadow of Man,* she wrote, "How lucky I was to have a mother like Vanne. She was one in a million. I could not have done without her during those early days. She ran the clinic and ensured the goodwill of my neighbors. She kept the camp neat . . . and above all, she helped me to keep up my spirits during the depressing weeks when I could get nowhere near the chimps."

Jane went on to explain how hard her mother's life had been at the time. Since there was no refrigerator, they ate mostly baked beans, corned beef, and other kinds of canned foods. Jane also recalled two times when her mother had woken up to find a deadly giant centipede hanging right over her head!

❖

"How lucky I was to have a mother like Vanne. She was one in a million. I could not have done without her during those early days."

A New Routine

After five months, Jane's mother had to return to England. At first Jane felt lonely without her. As the weeks passed, however, she became so busy with work that there was no time to be lonely. Getting up each morning before six o'clock, she would eat a banana and drink a cup of coffee. Then she would climb the steep slope behind the camp and head into the forest. Stuffed in her pockets were a small pair of binoculars, a camera, a notebook, small ends of pencils, a handful of raisins for lunch, and plastic bags in case it rained.

Most often Jane would return to the camp after the sun had already set. She would eat a small meal of beans, tomatoes, and an egg and would then sit by the light of the campfire. Sometimes, for several more hours, she would write out the notes she had taken during the day. Often it was midnight before she had finished. Then she would go to bed—only to get up and follow the same routine the next day and each day after that.

Jane followed this routine even during the rainy season. In Africa, the rainy season begins in October or November and lasts until April or May. During this time, skies remain mostly gray. Downpours are

common, sometimes lasting as long as 12 hours. On the few days when there is sun, the air becomes thick and steamy—like a tropical greenhouse.

At Gombe, Jane often put in 16-hour days of tireless research and note taking. On a typical day, she was up at dawn and in bed after midnight.

As the rainy season continues, the grass shoots up until it is more than 12 feet high in some places. This tall grass made Jane's work much harder. First, the grass made it difficult to find any tracks. And even if Jane found some, she could not follow them for long. Then, because she could not see above the tall grass, she sometimes got lost. The only solution at such times was to climb a tree and look around.

There were also periods during the rainy season when the tall grass was constantly wet. Later Jane wrote, "There were times when I seemed to be wet through for days on end. I think I spent some of the coldest hours of my life in those mountains, sitting in clammy clothes in an icy wind looking for chimpanzees."

However, when everything around her was wet, Jane could walk through the forest more quickly. Still, she could not get close to the chimpanzees. Each day her panic grew more. She was afraid she would be sent back if she could not soon begin to observe the chimps more closely. Then one morning she looked up at the mountain that rose directly behind the camp. It was the same mountain she had climbed her first day there. Immediately, she knew she had to climb it again.

In order to earn the trust of the African chimpanzees, Jane had to be patient. In time, the animals grew eager to share in her company.

The climb up the steep mountain was very difficult. A few times, Jane even had to stop to catch her breath. Eventually, though, she reached the top, which rose about 1,000 feet above Lake Tanganyika. Jane had forgotten how much she could see from up there. She decided to stay the whole day and look for chimpanzees through her binoculars.

The Start of a Relationship

Within 15 minutes, a slight movement beyond a narrow ravine caught her eye. As she adjusted her binoculars, she saw three chimps standing there. To her amazement, she realized they were staring right at her! Even though she was sitting very still, she expected them to run away. But they did not move for several more minutes. Then they calmly walked into some thick vegetation. Jane's heart was pounding rapidly. This had been the first time that chimpanzees had seen her and had not run away!

Later that morning a group of chimps noisily came down the opposite mountain slope. They began to eat the figs on some trees that were growing there. About 20 minutes later, another group of chimps came from a different direction. Seeing her on top of the mountain, the second group of chimps stopped. As they stared at her, they let out a few loud calls. Then they joined the other chimps and calmly began to eat the figs as well. Again Jane could not believe that they had not run away in panic.

After a while, all the chimps climbed down from the fig trees and went off in a group. From her position on top of the mountain, Jane could see them very well. She watched as they walked in a long, orderly line—one following another. She also noticed that two small chimps were riding on their mothers' backs. Before they disappeared into the grass, she saw them stop to take a drink at a small stream.

Recalling that experience, Jane wrote, "It was by far the best day I had had since my arrival at Gombe . . . . That day, in fact, marked the turning point in my study." She explained that the chimps returned to eat the figs for the next eight weeks. As a result, they got used to seeing her each day at the same place. During that time she never followed them, and she never disturbed them in any way. And finally, after such a long time, they began to trust her. As Jane later said, "Eventually they got used to this peculiar, white-skinned ape and became less fearful of me."

After several weeks, she carried a small tin trunk up to the peak. In it she kept a kettle, some coffee, a few cans of baked beans, a sweater, and a blanket. Many times the chimps slept near the fig trees. When they did, she wanted to be able to stay up on the peak overnight. Then when she awoke, she would be able to see them first thing in the morning.

Chimp Nests and Names

One of the most amazing things Jane observed during those weeks on the peak was the way the chimps made nests, or beds, in the trees at night. One evening, for example, Jane watched while David Graybeard made his nest. First he looked for a sturdy foundation. Usually this was two or three branches that came together in the shape of a fork. When he found a good foundation, he stood in the center of it and bent down a number of the smaller branches from each side. With swift movements, he placed the leafy ends across the foundation. With his feet, he held all of these in place. Then with his hands, he bent in all the little leafy twigs that stuck around the nest. Finally his nest was ready—in just about three minutes. But something must have been wrong. He

"Eventually they got used to this peculiar, white-skinned ape and became less fearful of me."

After long months of observation, Jane realized that chimps are as different from one another as humans are.

seemed to be uncomfortable. After lying in it for a few minutes, he abruptly sat up. Then he grabbed another handful of leafy twigs, put them under his head, and happily settled down for the night.

Jane noticed that all the chimps made their own nests—except the young ones. Up to the age of three, chimps shared a nest with their mothers. Since chimps are constantly moving from place to place, they make a new nest each night. Sometimes, after the chimps left their nests, Jane would climb up the trees to look at them more closely. She was often amazed to see how cleverly the branches had been woven together.

During those months of observing the chimps from the peak, Jane also realized they are as different from one another as people are. She began to give them names. Years later she was asked how she chose the names. She answered, "Some names—such as Mrs. Maggs, Spray, and Mr. Worzle—simply came to mind. Strange as it may sound, some chimpanzees reminded me of friends or acquaintances in some gesture or manner, and I named them accordingly." Other chimps, of course, were named for other reasons. One chimp, for example, stood out from all the others because he was bald. He looked like the old gardener in the Peter Rabbit books, so Jane called him Mr. McGregor. Another chimp with a pale face gave Jane a creepy feeling the first time she saw him. Because of that, she appropriately named him Count Dracula. Within a short time, Jane had given names to about 50 of the chimpanzees.

Chapter 3

Acceptance

For nearly two months, Jane observed chimps from the mountain peak. Then she slowly and cautiously moved down the mountain to be closer to them. Soon she noticed that the chimps were more curious about her than they were afraid. But that curiosity quickly turned to unmistakable boldness. Instead of running away like before, they would climb into the trees, rock the branches, and stare at her in silence. This went on for several months.

The Excitement of Danger

At one time during those months, Jane decided to follow a group of chimpanzees through a thick part of the forest. As she stopped to get her bearings, she heard a branch snap right beside her. As she swung around, she saw a young chimp sitting in a tree almost directly over her head. Then she saw two females nearby.

Suddenly she realized that chimps were all around her—she was surrounded!

Jane sat down and tried to remain still. Then she heard a low "huh" sound in the thick vegetation to her right. Soon another "huh" came from behind her, and another from in front of her. These nervous chimpanzee calls continued for approximately 10 minutes. But Jane would only occasionally catch a glimpse of a large hand or a pair of glaring eyes.

Suddenly the calls grew louder, until the chimps were almost screaming. Then six large males rushed out of their hiding places. As each chimp became excited, he shook nearby tree branches and snapped off twigs. One chimp, named Goliath for his great size and strength, even climbed on a bush near Jane. She could see his hair standing on end as he wildly swayed back and forth. At one point, she thought he was going to land on top of her. Jane later confessed, "I think I expected to be torn to pieces."

Then, just as quickly as this display of anger had begun, it ended. Quietly, the males joined the females and their young and left. Years later, Jane wrote, "My knees were shaking when I got up. But there was the sense of excitement that comes when

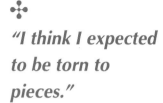

"I think I expected to be torn to pieces."

danger has come and left one unharmed. And the chimpanzees were surely less afraid of me now."

Another Frightening Experience

Another time, however, Jane was not so lucky. She was waiting for some chimps to pass by a ripe fruit tree when she heard footsteps in the leaves behind her. Trying not to scare the chimps, she lay down on the ground. When the footsteps got closer, they stopped. Then Jane heard a worried "Hoo! Hoo!" from one of the chimps.

Like a flash of lightning, a large male jumped into the tree directly over her. Soon the chimp started to show his rage by hitting the tree's trunk and shaking its branches wildly. His hoots became louder, until he was uttering high-pitched screams of anger. Overcome by fear, Jane remained motionless.

All at once the angry chimp seemed to disappear into the thick vegetation. After a moment of silence, however, he rushed toward Jane and let out a horrifying and brutal scream. She suddenly felt his hand slam down on the back of her head. Though dazed and fearful, she slowly sat up and looked around. When the chimp saw her move, he quickly ran off.

(Opposite page)
During her research at Gombe, Jane occasionally encountered angry chimps. Although those times were frightening and dangerous for her, she never failed to learn from the experiences and continue with her research.

Later she guessed that he must not have recognized her, because she was lying down. The plastic sheet she was wearing to protect herself against the rain also could have confused him. When she discussed this incident with Dr. Leakey, he said, "If you had waved your arms, shouted, or shown anger in any way, you might have been killed. He was merely testing to find out if you were an enemy or not." Dr. Leakey must have been right, because gradually over the next several months, the apes became less aggressive. In fact, Jane was eventually greeted almost as if she were a chimpanzee herself. Sometimes the chimps would show excitement by hooting and shaking the branches. At other times, they showed no interest in her at all.

Physical Contact

Although the chimps no longer seemed to be afraid of Jane, she was still not able to establish any personal relationships with them. That changed, however, one day about a year after her arrival in Gombe. On that day, Jane was sitting near David Graybeard by a tiny stream in the forest. On the ground she saw a ripe red palm nut. Slowly she picked it up and held it out to him on her open palm. At first he

With time, Jane began to develop special personal relationships with some of the Gombe chimps. When she followed David Graybeard, for example, he would often wait for her if she fell behind.

turned his head away. But Jane moved a little closer to him. Once again she held out her hand. This time he looked at the fruit, at Jane, and then back at the fruit. He reached out his hand and held her hand firmly but gently. After a moment, he released her hand and watched the nut drop to the ground.

"At that moment I didn't need a scientist to explain what had happened," Jane later wrote in her notes. "David Graybeard had communicated with me. It was as if he had said, 'Everything is going to be okay.' And for those few seconds, the wall between human and chimpanzee was broken down. It was a reward far beyond my greatest hopes." David had become the first chimpanzee to fully accept Jane.

That moment was the start of a deep and caring friendship between Jane and David. Once she wrote that she used to try to follow David in those early days. But it was often hard for her to keep up with him. Years later, she recalled, "Sometimes, I am sure, he waited for me—just as he would wait for Goliath or William. When I finally would break through the thorny undergrowth, I often found him sitting, looking back in my direction. Then he would get up and plod on again."

As her research progressed, Jane discovered that chimps build complex and unique relationships with one another—just like people.

Chapter 4

Great Discoveries

 During her first year at the Gombe Stream Game Reserve, Jane made two very important discoveries about the eating habits and abilities of chimps. Jane's first discovery occurred one day shortly after she had begun observing the chimps from the peak of the mountain. She made her second discovery quite by accident.

A Meaty Meal

One day as Jane was taking her daily walk, she was struck by the sounds of chimps up in a large tree. She looked up and, through her binoculars, she could see that a large male was holding something pink. From time to time, he would pull pieces from it with his teeth. A female and her baby were reaching out, begging for whatever it was that he had.

Then it dawned on Jane. The chimp was eating a small dead monkey! Up to this time, many had believed that chimpanzees ate only vegetables. Others believed that chimps might occasionally kill and eat a small lizard or rodent. However, no one had thought that chimps would kill another fairly large animal just to eat it.

It was not until several years later that Jane actually saw a chimp track and kill another animal. It happened as she was watching four red monkeys resting in a tree. From out of nowhere, a young chimpanzee suddenly appeared. One of the monkeys saw him but did not run away, thinking that the chimp wasn't moving any closer. However, as the monkey kept its eye on the first chimp, a second chimp raced up the tree. With tremendous speed, he shot across the branch, grabbed the monkey, and broke its neck.

Immediately five other chimpanzees climbed up the tree. Without any fighting, the monkey was torn apart, and each chimp got a piece. Later Jane explained that the monkey was shared because it had been caught by a young male. However, there is little sharing when an adult male kills an animal. At such times, the other chimps sit close around the chimp with the meat. Even though they show great respect by not trying to take any of it, the

❖

Jane made two very important discoveries about the eating habits and abilities of chimps.

younger chimps do look longingly and hold out their hands—palm side up—as if they are begging for a piece.

Although chimps enjoy an occasional piece of meat, they mainly eat vegetables. In fact, Jane collected 81 different kinds of fruits, leaves, seeds, blossoms, stems, and barks that were most frequently eaten by the chimps during her first year at the Gombe Reserve.

Chimp Tools

One rainy morning, Jane was feeling very discouraged. She had trudged through the forest for hours and had not seen a single chimp. Just as she was about to climb to the peak, she saw a chimp bent over a termite nest.

Quickly, she sat down and pulled out her binoculars. Even from behind she could recognize the familiar shape of David Graybeard. But for a few minutes she could not understand what he was doing. Then she realized he was trimming the edges of a wide blade of sword grass. But why was he doing that? Jane watched some more. When David had finished, he stuck the narrow blade of grass into the termite nest. He sat for a few minutes and then pulled it out and stuck it into his mouth.

After repeating this action several times, David turned the blade of grass over. Seeing that it was bent, he threw it away. Then he reached over and pulled out a piece of vine from the ground. Holding onto it with one hand, he stripped the leaves off with the other. After biting off a piece at the end, he put the vine into the mound and began the process again.

Jane watched him for more than an hour. He moved only when he opened up new holes in the termite mound. He did this by scraping away the thin outer layer of soil

Perhaps Jane's greatest discovery was that chimps make and use their own tools—like this blade of grass used as a termite catcher. Before Jane's research was made public, scientists had believed that humans were the only animals capable of such skills.

with his index finger. After eating—and obviously enjoying—many more termites, David finally got up and walked away.

When he was out of sight, Jane ran over to the termite mound and watched as many worker termites closed up the holes David had made. Finally, she picked up one of the vines herself and stuck it into the mound. Immediately she could feel several termites bite into it. When she pulled it out, six were still holding on. Jane knew that she had discovered something incredible.

✤

Unable to hold in her excitement any longer, Jane ran back to camp to write to Dr. Leakey. She had discovered that chimps not only used tools, but they also made them!

Unable to hold in her excitement any longer, Jane ran back to camp to write to Dr. Leakey. She had discovered that chimps not only *used* tools, but they also *made* them! Up until then, the majority of scientists had defined humans as the only creatures who were capable of creating and using their own tools.

There had been cases of animals using tools before. Sea otters, for example, get a flat stone from the ocean floor and use it to open shellfish on their stomachs. But no one had ever before seen an animal make a tool for a specific purpose!

Dr. Leakey quickly wrote back. He said that, based on Jane's discovery, he believed scientists now had three choices. "They

Some of Jane's most interesting discoveries had to do with the tools chimps made for eating. Here, a chimp uses a handful of leaves as a cup for drinking water.

must accept chimps as man, they must redefine man, or they must redefine tools."

A year following this discovery, Jane saw chimps create another tool. She watched as a young chimp pulled off all the leaves of a branch. He stuck them into his mouth and chewed them for a few minutes. Then he reached into his mouth with his index and middle fingers and pulled out a small wad of chewed leaves. He dunked the wad into a pool of water. Then after pulling it out, he sucked the water from the leaves. "Of course," Jane thought to herself, "he's just created a homemade sponge!"

Chapter 5

Bananas

One day, as Jane was returning to the camp, Dominic, the cook, ran up to her with some exciting news. He was anxious to report that a chimp had come into the camp that morning. The chimp had seemed unfearful and had stayed about an hour, eating the fruits in the palm tree over Jane's tent. After the chimp had returned for several days in a row, Jane decided it was time to wait for him.

Around ten o'clock one morning, she heard a movement. When she looked up from her work, she saw the familiar shape of David Graybeard as he strolled calmly past the front of her tent. For the next hour, she could hear occasional grunts of pleasure as he ate the red fruit in the tree. After he climbed down, he deliberately looked inside Jane's tent before he headed back into the forest. As long as there was fruit on the tree, David returned to the camp each day. Although Jane did not remain at camp too many days, she did find several excuses to wait for him. She later wrote, "Sometimes, though, I waited for him to come just for the great pleasure of seeing him so close and so unafraid."

On one of those days, Jane was working at a table outside her tent. After David came down from the tree, he walked over to her. When he stopped about five feet away from her, Jane watched as the hair all over his body suddenly began to stand on end. This happens to chimps when they become angry or nervous. With their hair puffed out, they look huge and mean. Before she had a chance to become afraid, David charged toward her. He grabbed a banana from her table and ran off with it. From that time on, Jane asked Dominic to leave bananas around for David and any other chimps that came into the camp.

Before she had a chance to become afraid, David charged toward her.

A Partner

In 1962, about a year after Jane had been at the reserve, a man named Hugo Van Lawick arrived at the camp. He had been sent there by the National Geographic Society. His assignment was to take photographs and make a film of Jane and her work with the chimpanzees. Like Jane, he

Jane met her first husband, photographer Hugo Van Lawick, in 1962. Together, the couple shared a deep love for the animals of Africa.

had always loved animals. He had also become a photographer in hopes that he would someday get to Africa to film wild animals. With so much in common, Jane and Hugo soon fell in love and were married in London in 1964.

After taking only a three-day honeymoon, the two hurried back to Africa. They were both anxious to see the new baby of one of the chimps. It was going to be Jane's first opportunity to observe a newborn chimp in the wild. Also, the rainy season had already begun, and they wanted to get back to the reserve before the rains became too heavy. However, by the time they arrived in Nairobi, many of the roads were already closed. But they had hope—they had a Land Rover with four-wheel drive. When they learned they could still get through to the reserve on one route, they left at once.

After they had gone more than three fourths of the way, they came to a road that was too flooded to pass and had to turn back. But would they even be able to get back? The two rivers they had already crossed had been near flood stage hours before. They easily could have already overflowed their banks! Jane later remembered Hugo saying, "If either of the other rivers rises much, we shall really be stuck. We may not be able to cross for days, or even weeks—perhaps not until the end of the rainy season."

Driving as fast as they could, the couple eventually reached the first bridge. Since the road turned as it connected with the bridge, Jane had to jump out of the Land Rover and use her body to mark the bend in the road. She was knee-deep in water. Then as Hugo drove by, she splashed through the water and jumped into the car.

Three dark, treacherous miles later, they finally reached the second river, which was dangerously high. "Shall we risk it?" her husband asked. When Jane nodded yes,

Hugo stepped on the accelerator, and they drove as fast as they could. About halfway across, the engine hesitated. At the same moment, their wheels began to slip sideways on the flooded bridge. Just as they thought the strong river current was going to sweep them over the edge, the engine started up again! Almost miraculously, they made it to the other side. But they still had to drive another 100 miles back to Nairobi. Eventually they got to the game reserve by train.

Outsmarting the Chimps

Once Jane and her husband were back, they decided to set up a permanent feeding station at their camp. Having the chimps so close by would help both of them with their work. Jane would be able to observe the chimps more closely, and Hugo would be able to take some wonderful pictures of them.

Before they had even figured out how to set up the feeding station, they had to build a second storage area for the many bushels of bananas they had collected. Just a few days before, one of the natives had built a structure of strong wooden bars, covered with thick grass. He had assured Jane that the storage area was chimp-proof.

However, they all watched helplessly as David Graybeard made a hole in the roof within just a few minutes. He climbed in, and after eating about 60 bananas, he climbed out. Although he was obviously stuffed, he dragged out a large bunch of bananas and staggered off into the forest. An aluminum building was immediately erected to keep the bananas safe.

The feeding station itself posed many problems. The biggest problem was coming up with a system that would prevent the older chimps from taking the bananas away from the younger chimps. Jane and her helpers began with individual boxes.

Ever since childhood, Jane knew her home would eventually be in Africa—among the wild animals that she loved so much.

But the chimps were much smarter than expected. Both the old and the young soon learned how to open each lock with either intelligence or sheer strength. Chimps were constantly in one another's boxes.

Jane finally decided on concrete boxes with steel lids. The lids were held shut by wires threaded through underground pipes. These wires were then attached to levers some distance away. When the levers were released, the wires became loose, and the lids fell open. In the short time, however, even the young chimps figured out how to open these boxes. As a result, Jane had to install an electrical system to operate them. Although perfecting this system took more than six years, Jane did not mind. She never tired of watching how cleverly the chimps solved problems.

Beyond Food

As more and more chimps started to come to the camp, Jane's problems grew. Although the chimps would come mostly for bananas, they soon found that they liked other things just as much—blankets and pieces of clothing, for example. Sometimes Jane would find blankets in the forest. Or she would see the chimps chewing on a sweater or a dirty sock. As a result, the staff had to securely lock all these items in metal boxes.

When the chimps could no longer find any clothes, they began to chew on canvas chairs and shoes. And when the shoes and chairs got locked up, the chimps began gnawing on the tents themselves. In fact, one day when Jane returned from the forest, she had a big surprise. She found three chimps sitting in the middle of what used to be her tent. All that was left was her metal frame and a few pieces of canvas.

With so many chimps coming into the camp, Jane hired Edna Koning, her first research assistant. Edna's main job was to type Jane's notes. Edna, of course, ended up helping in many other ways as well. When the number of chimps visiting the camp reached 45, Jane hired her second assistant, Sonia Ivey. Nine years later, Jane would employ more than 10 students. Jane later wrote, "When I first set foot on the sandy beach of the Gombe Stream Chimpanzee Reserve, I never imagined that I was taking the first step toward the establishment of the Gombe Stream Research Centre." By then, Jane had also earned her Ph.D. (an advanced academic degree) from Cambridge University in England.

One day when Jane returned from the forest, she had a big surprise. She found three chimps sitting in the middle of what used to be her tent.

Mother-Love

In 1966, the population at the research center increased by one more. Jane and Hugo became the proud parents of a baby boy. From the very beginning, he was nicknamed Grub. Jane later explained that having a baby of her own helped her better understand the lives of the chimps: "Until I had an infant of my own, I could not begin to understand the basic, powerful instinct of mother-love. For example, if someone accidentally frightened Grub, I would get angry. After experiences like this, I could more easily understand the feelings of chimpanzee mothers. They would angrily wave their arms to threaten anyone who came too close to their infants, or at a playmate who accidentally hurt their children."

Jane applied some of the child-rearing techniques that she had observed in the chimps to her own child. For example, she provided Grub a great deal of physical contact and affection, and she played with him a lot. She and her husband also took him everywhere they went.

As Grub grew older, Jane and Hugo had to seriously consider his safety. They knew that chimpanzees had been known to take and eat human infants. And to prevent

❖

"Until I had an infant of my own, I could not begin to understand the basic, powerful instinct of mother-love."

anything from happening, they built a cage for Grub. Remembering those early years, Grub has said, "If you raise your eyebrows and stare at [the chimps], it's like a threat. Of course, if you're safe in a cage, it's quite fun—they will come and bang on it. But they remember you, and when they see you outside, they will come for you." When Grub turned nine, Jane sent him off to a boarding school in England.

Two Losses

During those years, Jane missed her son very much. But she also missed her friend, David Graybeard, who had stopped coming to camp altogether. Although they never found his body, they knew that he had died. When Jane finally accepted the fact, she wrote, "Of all the Gombe chimpanzees, it is David Graybeard whom I have loved the most."

In 1974, Jane had to make yet another major adjustment. She and Hugo separated and divorced. Those who knew Jane guessed that the couple had simply spent too much time together. As one friend said, "They worked together twenty-four hours a day and shared the same tent year after year with no communication with other people. It was too much."

Chapter 6

A Turning Point

 In 1975—14 years after Jane had first gone to Gombe—everything changed. One night, 40 armed men kidnapped 4 student workers at the research center. For days no one at the center knew where the students had been taken, or if they were even alive.

Jane and the other students waited for word from the kidnappers in a house in Dar es Salaam in Tanzania. The house belonged to Derek Bryceson, Jane's new husband of only a few months. She had gotten to know him because he was the director of the national parks in Tanzania. Like her first husband, he also shared her great love of wild animals.

After about a week—which seemed more like a month—one of the students who had been kidnapped was sent back with a ransom demand. Jane later recalled, "I shall never forget the relief, the great joy, that I experienced on learning that the four were alive." Unfortunately, however, because the issues involved were all political, the negotiations went on for a long time.

Finally, the ransom was paid, but one student was held back after the others had been freed. Again Jane anxiously waited and worried for both the student and the student's family. Then, after another two weeks, the last student hostage was released.

During the hostage ordeal, Jane had made a couple of short trips back to the research center. She had wanted to show support for the members of the local field staff. They had continued to keep the records on the chimps during the ordeal. Now that it was over, Jane had to figure out the fate of the research center. Only one decision was easy to make. She would no longer have any foreign students working at the center.

One night, 40 armed men kidnapped 4 student workers at the research center.

Passing On the Work

Eventually, with the help of her husband, Jane persuaded the members of the local field staff to continue the work at the research center on their own. Actually, for several years they had been doing much of the work anyway. They had learned to

After four of her assistants were taken hostage in 1975, Jane realized that it was no longer safe for foreign students to stay at Gombe. As a result, local field workers took on the research and observation responsibilities of the students.

follow the chimps and chart their daily movements, groupings, and even their food intake. Nevertheless, they had looked to the students and Jane for a certain amount of help and direction. Jane later wrote, "Now it was necessary to convince them that they could carry on without us."

Throughout the following weeks, Jane worked closely with them. Mostly she gave them the confidence needed to continue her work. Eventually, the local workers divided into two teams. Each team would follow a different target chimpanzee for as long as possible on a given day. One would record the behavior of the chimp, and the other would mark the chimp's route, list the food, and keep track of any other chimps that the target chimp came in contact with. When Jane visited the camp, all of her field workers would sit around a fire on the beach at night. There, they would tell her everything they had learned.

Five years later, when her husband died of cancer, Jane was overwhelmed with sadness. But even during this difficult time, she realized how her sorrow would help her to better understand the chimps. She wrote, "After the death of my second husband, terrible grief came over me. But only then did I even begin to understand how young chimps can pine away and die when they lose their mothers."

After spending some time with her family in England, Jane returned to Gombe. "There," she wrote, "I could hide my hurt among the ancient trees and find new strength for living in the forests." During the many hours she spent in the forests of Gombe at that time, she took few notes on the chimps. Still, she felt that she had never been closer to them. She later guessed that the reason was quite simple. It was the first time she had ever really "needed" to be near them.

Championing the Rights of Chimps

After her husband's death, Jane realized that she needed to broaden her work with the chimpanzees. "For years I was selfishly concerned only with the Gombe chimps," she once said. "Now, I'm worried about the treatment and survival of chimps everywhere."

As a result, she founded the Jane Goodall Institute in Tucson, Arizona, in 1977. The purpose of the institute is to help save the world's dwindling chimpanzee population. Poaching, hunting, and the destruction of chimpanzee habitats have caused the world population of chimps to drop to 175,000.

In 1977, Jane founded the Jane Goodall Institute in Tucson, Arizona. Through education and fund-raising efforts, the institute works to help save the world's decreasing chimpanzee population.

Since 1977, Jane has been lecturing one month a year at the institute. She also spends much of her time raising money throughout the world for her cause.

Over the years, Jane's deep concern for chimpanzees has extended to those kept in zoos or as pets or amusements for tourists. "Chimps are thinking, feeling beings," Jane has told many audiences, "and yet they face extinction because of human ignorance, greed, and neglect."

Whenever possible, Jane also visits chimps that are kept in laboratories for research on diseases such as AIDS. Over the years, more and more chimps have been used for experimental purposes. This has occurred because scientists have discovered that chimpanzees are more like humans than any other living creatures.

Jane has sadly accepted the need for chimps in medical research, at least until there is an alternative. But she constantly campaigns for better conditions for the chimps in the laboratories. "The suffering of chimps can be reduced by putting them in bigger cages, exposing them to the outdoors, and allowing them more contact with each other," she has stressed during her tours. "Toys and even simple video games can relieve the deadly boredom you

"For years I was selfishly concerned only with the Gombe chimps. Now I'm worried about the treatment and survival of chimps every- where."

see in all those empty stares." Fortunately, a number of researchers have begun to follow some of her suggestions.

At the end of many of her lectures and talks, Jane usually tells the story about an eight-year-old chimp named Old Man. At the zoo, he was placed on a human-made island with three females. After he had been there for several years, a young man named Marc Cusano was hired to feed the chimps. He was warned at the time not to go near them. "Those brutes are vicious," he was told. "They'll kill you."

Although he was cautious at first, Marc soon started going closer and closer to the chimps. One day, while he was sitting in his boat, Old Man reached out and gently took a banana from Marc's hand. At that moment Marc and Old Man began a very special friendship that just kept growing. Eventually, Marc even groomed and played with Old Man.

One day when Marc slipped and fell, he startled an infant chimp. Screaming, the infant ran to its mother. To protect her baby, the mother instinctively leaped on Marc and bit his neck. As he lay there, the other two females rushed up and joined in the attack. Then, just when Marc thought he was going to die, Old Man charged

(Opposite page)
Jane's passionate work on behalf of African chimpanzees has not slowed down. She continues to lecture, lobby, and work tirelessly to improve conditions for chimps all over the world.

toward the three females. He pushed them away and stayed close to Marc. With Old Man's help, Marc was finally able to get into his boat and row away to safety. There is no question in Marc's mind that Old Man saved his life.

Jane Goodall concludes the story with the following challenge. "If a chimpanzee—one, moreover, who has been abused by humans—can reach out across the species barrier to help a human friend in need, then surely we, with our deeper capacity for compassion and understanding, can reach out to help the chimpanzees who need us, so desperately, today. Can't we?"

Glossary

Explaining New Words

consciousness The state of being awake and alert.

extinct No longer in existence; killed off.

field-worker A researcher who goes out and gathers information through first-hand observation.

game Wild animals who are sought after by hunters and poachers. Reserves, or safe havens, are often established to try to protect these animals.

habitat An environment in which an organism or group of organisms lives naturally.

hostage A person held against his or her will. Usually, hostage-taking is used to illegally influence the actions of another person or party.

malaria A serious disease, sometimes fatal, that is carried by certain mosquitoes in Africa. It is often characterized by periods of chills and fever.

poacher A person who kills or catches wild animals illegally.

prehistoric Relating to the period of time before recorded history.

rainy season In Africa, the period from October until May when it rains nearly all the time. During the few days that it is sunny, the air becomes thick and steamy—like a tropical greenhouse.

ransom Something demanded, usually a large sum of money, in return for a person or group of persons taken hostage.

species A group of organisms that share many traits with one another and that can reproduce with one another.

vegetation Plant life.

For Further Reading

Birnbaum, Bette. *Jane Goodall and the Wild Chimpanzees.* Madison, NJ: Raintree Steck-Vaughn, 1989.

Darling, David. *Could You Ever Speak Chimpanzee?* New York: Dillon, 1991.

Fromer, Julie. *Jane Goodall: Living with the Chimps.* New York: Twenty-First Century Books, 1992.

Goodall, Jane. *The Chimpanzee Family Book.* Saxonville, MA: Picture Book Studio, 1991.

Goodall, Jane. *Jane Goodall's Animal World: Gorillas.* New York: Aladdin, 1990.

Goodman, Billy. *Animal Homes and Societies.* Boston: Little, Brown & Co., 1992.

Lucas, Eileen. *Jane Goodall: Friend of the Chimps.* Brookfield, CT: Millbrook Press, 1992.

McCormick, Maxine. *Chimpanzee.* New York: Crestwood House, 1990.

Index

Photo Credits:
Cover and title page: ©Gerry Ellis/The Wildlife Collection; p. 4: ©P. Breese/
Gamma-Liaison; p. 5: ©Lawrence Migdale/Gamma-Liaison; p. 7: ©Gerry Ellis/The
Wildlife Collection; p. 9: AP/Wide World Photos; p. 13: AP/Wide World Photos;
p. 15: ©Gerry Ellis/The Wildlife Collection; p. 17: Bildarchiv OKAPIA/Photo
Researchers, Inc.; p. 19: ©P. Breese/Gamma-Liaison; p. 23: ©P. Breese/Gamma-
Liaison; p. 24: ©P. Breese/Gamma-Liaison; p. 28: ©Tom McHugh/Photo Re-
searchers, Inc.; p. 30: AP/Wide World Photos; p. 33: ©P. Breese/Gamma-Liaison;
p. 34: ©Gerry Ellis/The Wildlife Collection; p. 35: ©Hugo Van Lawick/Courtesy
Jane Goodall Institute; p. 36: ©Ray Ellis/Photo Researchers, Inc.; p. 39: ©Gerry
Ellis/The Wildlife Collection; p. 41: ©Tom McHugh/Photo Researchers, Inc.; p.
42: ©Tom McHugh/Photo Researchers, Inc.; p. 44: AP/Wide World Photos; p. 47:
©P. Breese/Gamma-Liaison; p. 52: ©Gerry Ellis/The Wildlife Collection; p. 54:
©Gerry Ellis/The Wildlife Collection; p. 56: Courtesy of the Jane Goodall Institute;
p. 58: AP/Wide World Photos.

Map on page 11 by Sandra Burr/©Blackbirch Press, Inc.